TOTALLY

Why is a president like a Thanksgiving dinner?
In both, a turkey is the centre of attention.

***

What are WASPs thankful for at Thanksgiving?
That the Pilgrim fathers weren't Polish.

***

What do Jewish kids want for Chanukah?
Christmas.

***

What made Rudolf's nose so red?
Brown-nosing Santa.

***

Why do they call it the North Pole?
Because Santa's well-hung.

***

What did the woman moan while having sex with St. Nicholas?
"Santa Claus is coming."

***

Why is New Year's Eve a special night for whores?
It's the one night they get to blow something else besides cocks.

***

If you're out parking after a New Year's Eve party, be careful. Accidents cause people.

The (Totally Outrageous) Season's Greetings Joke Book

Sidney "Scrooge" Spite

PaperJacks LTD.

TORONTO   NEW YORK

AN ORIGINAL

PaperJacks

The (Totally Outrageous) Season's Greetings Joke Book

PaperJacks LTD.

330 STEELCASE RD. E., MARKHAM, ONT. L3R 2M1
210 FIFTH AVE., NEW YORK, N.Y. 10010

PaperJacks edition published December 1986

This original PaperJacks edition is printed from brand-new plates made from newly set, clear, easy-to-read type. No part of this book may be reproduced or transmitted in any form or by any means, electronic or mechanical, including photography, recording, or any information storage or retrieval system, without permission in writing from the publisher.

....

To my second wife, Sarah N. Spite . . . who wants a divorce because she thought sex was for making babies and I thought it was for making jokes.

Contents

PART I
THANKSGIVING

Pilgrim Farters

Chapter One

Why would Thanksgiving be better for born-agains if the Pilgrims had killed bobcats instead of turkeys? At least they'd get to eat pussy *once* a year.

***

Why is it too bad the Indians didn't kill all the Pilgrims?
Because then we wouldn't have so many obnoxious WASPs running around.

***

How do we know the Pilgrims were good little preppies?
They liked to sail, they lived in Massachusetts, and they all dressed the same.

How do we know the Pilgrims liked to screw a lot?
Just think how many Americans claim their ancestors
came over on the *Mayflower*.

***

What was the Mayflower Compact?
The first foreign car import.

***

How do we know the Pilgrims were into pop music?
They got off on Plymouth Rock.

***

What's it called when a Pilgrim is shot full of arrows?
Holier than thou.

***

What's it called when Puritans steal Indian lands?
Pilgrim's Progress.

***

Why was the first Thanksgiving meal so asinine?
Think of it. A bunch of stuffed shirts stuffing their
faces with stuffed birds.

***

What should the Pilgrim Fathers really be called?
Pilgrim Farters: after they pigged out on the four
turkeys, they could be heard for miles around.

Why should Americans be pissed off at the Pilgrims? Think of all the dumb relatives we're forced to see every year.

Talking Turkey

Chapter Two

What do chickens and ducks have to be thankful for on Thanksgiving Day?
Turkeys.

***

What do you get when you cross George Bush with a Thanksgiving fowl?
A *real* turkey.

***

Who started the long nightmare for American turkeys?
Those first four dumb birds who let themselves be caught.

***

How do turkeys sense Thanksgiving is approaching?
They feel a sudden, sharp pain in the neck area.

How is a turkey like Ringo Starr?
They both have two drumsticks and no talent.

***

What's the difference between a Thanksgiving turkey
and a nympho?
One loses a head, the other gives it.

***

How is a turkey like a flight attendant?
They both fly and are good to eat.

***

How do turkeys view Thanksgiving?
Nothing to lose one's head over.

***

Why is a presidential press conference like a
Thanksgiving dinner?
In both, a turkey is the center of attention.

***

What do you call a Thanksgiving bird who informs
on his fellow fowls?
A stool turkey.

***

What do you call a Thanksgiving dinner for addicts?
A turkey shoot.

How can you tell if a turkey is Italian?
There's hair under its wings.

***

What does a meeting with Margaret Thatcher have in common with a bad Thanksgiving dinner?
They both involve a tough old bird.

***

What do you call a female turkey in a pen with 500 male turkeys?
Nervous.

***

Why didn't the turkey cooperate with the turkey farmer?
He didn't want to stick his neck out.

***

Who is never hungry at Thanksgiving dinner?
The turkey. He's stuffed.

***

Who was best dressed at the Salvation Army's Thanksgiving dinner?
The turkey.

***

A man decided to buy a live turkey for Thanksgiving dinner. As he was carrying the bird home, he passed a theatre where there was a movie playing he really wanted to see. The ticket taker said he couldn't bring the turkey in with him. He returned a few minutes later with the bird tucked down his pants and had no trouble getting in. As he was watching the show, the turkey stuck his head out of the man's fly and started to stare at a woman sitting in the next seat.

"This man has taken his cock out of his pants and it's pointing straight at me!" the upset woman told her husband.

"So, what's the big deal?" he asked. "You've seen that before."

Suddenly, the turkey began going, "Gobble, gobble."

"Maybe," said the woman, "But I've never been asked to give head by a talking prick!"

***

How is a well-cooked turkey like a leper?
On both, the meat falls off by itself.

***

How can you identify a Southern Californian turkey?
It stands up to surf in the microwave.

***

How did the dumb turkey survive the Thanksgiving slaughter?
He had his head up his ass.

What do you get when you cross a tom turkey with a tom turkey?
Two guilty tom turkeys.

***

How are a nerd's parents like a poultry farmer?
They both raise young turkeys.

***

How is Jesus like a Thanksgiving turkey?
Both stuck their necks out for mankind.

***

What's the difference between a Thanksgiving turkey and Moammar Khadafy?
One's stuffed, the other ought to be.

***

What's an alcoholic Thanksgiving bird?
A turkey on rye.

***

What's an alcoholic Thanksgiving bird that has just climaxed?
A turkey on rye with mayo.

***

Why did the cannibal eat a turkey on Thanksgiving?
He was fed up with people.

10

On Thanksgiving Day, while sitting in a park, a poor man and his wife were bemoaning the fact that they had no turkey for their Thanksgiving dinner. Two men carrying a huge cooked bird came by and heard what the couple were saying.

"If you let me and my friend fuck your wife, we'll give you this turkey," one of the men offered.

The man looked at his wife and she agreed. While she was having sex with the men in the nearby bushes, the husband sat and fondled the turkey in his hands. A policeman who had witnessed the whole scene came up to the husband.

"How can you let those two men fuck your wife like that?" the cop asked.

"A bird in the hand is worth two in the bush," the man replied.

***

What do turkeys call the fourth Friday in November?
1. *The Day After*.
2. The first day of the rest of their lives.

***

What do you call a turkey who makes it with roosters?
A cocksucker.

Food and Gluttony

Chapter Three

Why is Thanksgiving dinner like oral sex with an obese woman?
They both involve eating a fat bird.

***

How is a girl with bikini lines like a Thanksgiving dinner?
The white meat on both is more desirable.

***

Why is an integrated whorehouse like a traditional Thanksgiving dinner?
They both offer white and dark meat.

***

A college boy brought his girlfriend home for Thanksgiving dinner to meet his parents. Before dinner, the boy's father showed the girl the upstairs bedroom where she was to sleep. When they didn't return after twenty minutes or so, the boy's mother went up to investigate. She went into the bedroom and found the girl and the father screwing madly. She came downstairs.

"It's okay," she said, not wanting to upset her son, "Your father is just showing Sally his idea of a real Thanksgiving stuffing."

***

What's it called when a wife chews her husband's cock on Thanksgiving?
Minced meat.

***

What did Tip O'Neil say at the start of a Thanksgiving dinner?
"What! Only one turkey?"

***

What do you call stale, rotten bread in an Iranian jail?
Thanksgiving Dinner.

***

What do anorexics have for Thanksgiving dinner?
Enemas.

***

What do bulemics have for Thanksgiving dinner?
Two fingers.

What do speed freaks have for Thanksgiving dinner?
Fast food.

***

Why do surgeons like Thanksgiving dinner?
It's the one time of the year when they can cut into meat without worrying about being sued for malpractice.

***

Where do five menstruating lesbian chemical students eat Thanksgiving dinner?
At a periodic table.

***

Why is it so hard to tell the turkey from the host at a lesbian Thanksgiving dinner?
They both have their legs in the air.

***

What special dessert does a vampire family have at Thanksgiving dinner?
Used frozen sanitary napkins.

***

What special treat do poor senior citizens have on Thanksgiving?
Turkey-flavored Gravy Train.

***

What do you call Guiness Stout with boiled potatoes on the side?
A traditional Irish Thanksgiving dinner.

Why did the nerd baste his turkey with Coppertone?
He didn't want it to burn.

***

What do horny housewives use for stuffing?
Any oblong object they can get their hands on.

***

On their way home for Thanksgiving dinner, two men were flying over a desert. The plane crashed but the men survived. They were without food for days when they came upon the rotting carcass of a dead vulture. One man rushed up to the decaying bird, tore a piece off, and started to eat. The other man refused to do the same.

"I'm going to hold out for a hot Thanksgiving dinner," he said.

So the other man ate the entire dead buzzard. He soon became violently ill and vomited.

"Thank you, Lord," gleefully shouted the man who had not eaten, "For giving me this hot Thanksgiving bird!"

***

Why do Frenchmen love to put cranberry sauce on turkey?
It reminds them of oral sex.

***

What did the JAP make for Thanksgiving dinner?
Reservations.

Why is a Thanksgiving dinner on a camping trip like a Scotsman wearing a kilt?
They both involve a bird under a tent.

***

Why did the cannibals want to eat John Hinckley on Thanksgiving?
They wanted to have a traditional Thanksgiving dinner, complete with a *real* turkey.

***

Why is Thanksgiving a truly altruistic holiday for cannibals?
On that day they go out of their way to serve their fellow man.

***

Why did the moron chew razor blades before he sat down to Thanksgiving dinner?
He wanted to sharpen his appetite.

***

What's the quick and easy way to make a tossed salad for Thanksgiving dinner?
Feed two heads of lettuce, six carrots, six tomatoes, half a cup of oil, half a cup of vinegar, plus assorted spices to a bulemic. Then wait.

***

Did you hear about the moron's Thanksgiving dinner that really tickled his guests?
He forgot to pluck the turkey.

How is a girl in a low-cut gown like a Thanksgiving dinner?
Both have more meat than dressing.

***

What's the best thing to put in a homemade pumpkin pie?
Your teeth.

***

How can you tell Helen Keller at a Thanksgiving dinner?
She's the one with the drumstick in her ear.

***

At a nursing home Thanksgiving dinner, an elderly man's colostomy bag started to leak and ooze. "Darn," he said, "I hate to eat and run."

***

Where do they eat Thanksgiving dinner raw?
In a nudist colony.

***

The trouble with Thanksgiving dinner is that after you eat it, three days later you're hungry again.

Thanks a Lot

Chapter Four

What's worse than spending Thanksgiving with relatives?
Spending it with your cellmate.

***

Why didn't they let Tip O'Neil be grand marshal of the Macy's Thanksgiving Day Parade?
They didn't want the other giant inflated balloons to get jealous.

***

What are WASPs thankful for at Thanksgiving?
That the Pilgrim Fathers weren't Polish.

***

What are hippies thankful for at Thanksgiving?
A free meal from their parents.

What are yuppies thankful for at Thanksgiving?
They're not. They wanted to work that day.

***

What are fat people thankful for at Thanksgiving?
Guilt free eating.

***

What are bulemics thankful for at Thanksgiving?
Fingers.

***

What are old prison inmates thankful for at Thanksgiving?
Youthful offenders.

***

What are body shop owners thankful for at Thanksgiving?
Student drivers.

***

What are generals thankful for at Thanksgiving?
The chain of command.

***

What are Dolly Parton's fans thankful for at Thanksgiving?
Wide-angle lenses.

What are liberal gays thankful for at Thanksgiving?
White meat and dark meat.

***

What are plastic surgeons thankful for at Thanksgiving?
Windshields.

***

What are lawyers thankful for at Thanksgiving?
Clumsy doctors.

***

What are horny priests thankful for at Thanksgiving?
Choirboys.

***

What are horny nuns thankful for at Thanksgiving?
Crucifixes.

***

What are undertakers thankful for at Thanksgiving?
Drunk drivers.

***

What's Sylvester Stallone thankful for at Thanksgiving?
The public's bad taste.

What are blacks thankful for at Thanksgiving?
One night a year they don't have to eat chicken.

***

What are rednecks thankful for at Thanksgiving?
First cousins.

***

What are survivalists thankful for at Thanksgiving?
Uzis.

***

What are homeless people thankful for at
Thanksgiving?
Shopping bags.

***

What are bored housewives thankful for at
Thanksgiving?
Delivery boys.

***

What are rapists thankful for at Thanksgiving?
Ski masks.

***

What are nerds thankful for at Thanksgiving?
Kleenex.

What are nymphos thankful for at Thanksgiving?
Drumsticks.

***

What are Libyans thankful for at Thanksgiving?
Nothing.

***

What's Ronald Reagan thankful for at Thanksgiving?
The public's short memory.

***

What's the worst thing about Thanksgiving?
Less than four weeks till Christmas.

PART II
CHANUKAH

What and When and Why is Chanukah Anyway?

Chapter Five

Why is Hanukkah spelled Chanukah?
To confuse the unchosen.

***

Why is Chanukah like a low-calorie beer bash?
They're both a Festival of Lights.

***

What's hot, long, hard, and brings joy to JAPs?
New Chanukah candles.

***

What's the similarity between Chanukah candles and rock stars?
They both burn out eventually.

Why is an alcoholic like the first Chanukah candle?
They both stay lit a long time.

***

What do lit Chanukah candles and cocks have in common?
JAPs don't put their lips around either of them.

***

What do Palestinians light up on the last day of Chanukah?
Eight Israeli schoolbuses.

***

What Chanukah carol do Jewish kids sing?
"The Little Drummer Goy."

***

What do you call it when a JAP shaves her pussy for Chanukah?
Trimming the Chanukah bush.

***

What do you find growing on a Chanukah bush?
Pine Cohens.

***

How do blind Jews know when Chanukah is over?
They stop burning their fingers.

Chanukah Getting and Receiving

Chapter Six

What do Jewish kids want for Chanukah?
Christmas.

***

What kind of Chanukah presents do JAPs hate?
Ones without price tags.

***

What doll do Israeli boys get for Chanukah?
G.I. Jew.

***

What kind of doll makes a good Chanukah gift for
a little JAP?
One that walks, wets, and nags.

Why did the man give his wife a solid gold diaphragm for Chanukah?
He liked the idea of coming into money.

***

What cash gift do French Jews get at Chanukah?
Kosher francs.

***

What kind of doll do bitchy little JAPs get for Chanukah?
An On-the-Rag doll.

***

What did the man get his comatose JAP girlfriend for Chanukah?
Designer rubber sheets.

***

What kind of Teddy Ruxpin bear do JAPs get for Chanukah?
One that never stops talking.

***

Why did the man buy his JAP wife a black robe for Chanukah?
She reversed as many decisions as a Supreme Court judge.

What Chanukah gift can a JAP give her husband that will last forever?
A divorce.

***

What Chanukah gift do you get a JAP who always returns everything?
A boomerang.

***

Why do Jews like to get money at Chanukah?
Of all gifts, it's the easiest to exchange.

***

Why was the JAP so excited the day after Chanukah?
She could hardly wait to go out and exchange her gifts.

PART III
CHRISTMAS

Reindeer Hunting

Chapter Seven

What's invisible and smells like Christmas?
A reindeer fart.

***

What made Rudolf's nose so red?
Brown-nosing Santa.

***

Why do reindeer have small balls?
Most can't afford tuxedo rentals.

***

What's brown, horny, and has sore knees?
The head reindeer.

What do you call a reindeer with tire marks on his back?
Slow.

***

How does Santa make a slow reindeer fast?
He stops feeding him.

***

What do you call it when a reindeer jerks off on an evergreen tree?
Pining for love.

***

What do reindeer wear in bad weather?
Rein gear.

***

What do you call a reindeer with b.o.?
A reindeer sweater.

***

What kind of weather made Rudolf's red nose rot and fall off?
Acid rain.

***

Why does Santa let cocaine-addicted reindeer lead his sleigh during blizzards?
They're good snow blowers.

Why did the reindeer fuck the elf?
Reindeer are so horny they'll fuck anything.

***

Where are a reindeer's sex organs?
In his feet. If one steps on you, you're fucked.

***

Why is duck hunting more popular than reindeer hunting?
The decoys are easier to carry.

***

If Mr. and Mrs. Claus were Jewish, what would Rudolf be?
A fur coat.

***

When it's snowing, what's the difference between radial tires and reindeer?
Radial tires don't bleed when you put chains on them.

***

What's it called when a reindeer pisses in flight?
A yellow Christmas.

***

A cute female reindeer came running into Santa's workshop, bleeding from her pussy and said, "That's the last time I do it for fifty bucks."

Elves

Chapter Eight

Why do elves make good fairies?
Their mouths are just the right height.

***

What's it called when Santa leaves Mrs. Claus in charge of the the elves' workshop?
An orgy.

***

What did Mrs. Claus call the baldheaded elf?
Dildo.

***

What does a turnip have in common with a lobotomized elf?
They're both northern vegetables.

What does a gay elf with diarrhea have in common with a ripe grape?
They're both juicy little fruits.

***

What do you call a redheaded elf at the North Pole?
One of Mrs. Santa Claus's used tampons.

***

Who do the elves buy cocaine from at the North Pole?
Frosty the Snowman.

***

What do you get when you cross a reindeer with one of Santa's helpers?
A horny elf.

***

Why are there no black elves in Santa's shop?
They're all busy working as lawn jockeys.

***

What would happen if Santa Claus laid all his elves end to end?
He'd have a sore pecker.

***

Why was Mrs. Claus sexually dissatisfied after screwing the disagreeable elf?
He was a nasty little prick.

What word do elves use to describe fucking Mrs. Claus?
Spelunking.

***

What do you call Mrs. Claus's IUD?
An MIA elf.

***

What did the elf say after screwing Mrs. Claus?
"Why do *I* always have to sleep in the wet spot?"

***

Did you hear what Santa said to the elf who accidentally cut off his left hand while making toys?
"There, there, you'll be all right."

***

Santa was a tough boss around Christmas. He wanted the elves to work hard and not waste any time. He was so strict that he made the elves sign in and out every time they went to the toilet. One elf, fed up with this regimentation, went into the toilet, took off his wristwatch, put it in the bowl, then sat down. Santa came by the toilet after a few minutes, demanding to know why the elf was taking so long. He asked the elf to get up so he could verify if the elf was really doing anything legitimate. Santa was puzzled when he saw a watch in the middle of the pile.

"What's the meaning of this?" bellowed Santa.

"It's okay, Santa," the elf snidely replied, "I'm just shitting on my own time."

***

Why does Santa bury dead elves with their asses sticking above ground?
They're good for parking newly made bicycles.

***

What did Mrs. Santa say when her favorite elf got a frostbitten pecker?
"Oh boy . . . Ice pops!"

***

Why don't female elves wear tampons?
They trip over the strings.

***

What's small, cute, and scratches at the window?
An elf in a microwave.

The North Pole

Chapter Nine

Why do they call it the North Pole?
Because Santa's well-hung.

***

What happens when you step on the yellow line at the North Pole?
You get reindeer piss all over your shoes.

***

What low-calorie beers do elves drink?
Northern lights.

***

What vehicle does a door-to-door prostitute use at the North Pole?
A one-whore, open sleigh.

At the North Pole, where do Santa and his helpers keep their money?
Snowbanks.

***

How does Santa find the weather at the North Pole?
He goes outside and there it is.

***

What's the Ghost of Christmas Past when he visits Santa at his workshop?
North Pole-tergeist.

Santa Claus and the Missus

Chapter Ten

What's red and white and red and can't turn around in a chimney?
Santa with a spear in his back.

***

Why is the night before Christmas like being raped in prison?
They both involve a burly stranger going up your chimney.

***

What do Fidel Castro, the Smith Brothers, and Santa Claus have in common?
Girlfriends with chafed thighs.

Why is Santa like Jerry Falwell?
They're both involved in snow jobs.

***

What's red and white and glows in the dark?
Santa in the Ukraine.

***

Did you hear about Santa's identity crisis?
He didn't believe in himself.

***

While Santa was flying over the North Pole, an astronaut and a cosmonaut landed in his sleigh, victims of separate space disasters.

"Oh dear," said Santa, "I don't have room for both of you and all these toys. One of you will have to jump out."

To decide which one, Santa devised a little quiz. Whoever could answer two questions correctly could stay in the sleigh.

"Now," Santa asked the astronaut, "How many Wise Men were there in the nativity story?"

"That's easy," said the astronaut. "Three."

Then Santa asked the astronaut, "And how many camels?"

The astronaut again answered, "Three."

Then Santa turned to the Cosmonaut and said, "Okay, comrade, name the camels."

What's red and white and full of gunshot holes?
Santa in a bad neighborhood.

***

A boy and his little brother were playing on the roof of their house two weeks before Christmas. The smaller boy saw the chimney.

"Gee, can I go down the chimney like Santa Claus does?"

"Oh sure," the older brother replied, "Just climb in."

The little boy mounted the chimney and promptly fell into the darkness, screaming as he careened down the sides of the chimney, and breaking both his arms and legs. The boys' mother heard the screaming.

"What happened?" she screamed to the older brother on the roof.

"Oh", said the older boy, "I was just showing Junior that he's too old to believe in Santa Claus."

***

How come Santa is never on the Johnny Carson show?
There's no way Santa *and* Ed McMahon will fit on the same couch together.

***

When Santa had dysentery, what did he leave in some people's stockings?
Runs.

Why did the verbose cannibals eat Santa?
They wanted to chew the fat.

***

What's red and white and black and brown?
Santa being attacked by a Doberman.

***

What's the difference between regular Santa Claus
and Greek Santa Claus?
Regular Santa doesn't come in the back door.

***

Why is Santa so hip the day after Christmas?
He's a "beat" Nick.

***

What does Santa use to clean his teeth?
Santa Floss.

***

Why does Santa leave lots of presents in earthquake
zones?
He's generous to a fault.

***

What do elves eat while Santa is out delivering gifts
on Christmas Eve?
Mrs. Claus.

A little girl went to visit Santa at a department store. She sat on Santa's lap.

"Want to see my Magic Puppet?" Santa asked.

"Sure," the little girl replied.

Santa unbuttoned his fly and took out his prick.

"Now, if you kiss and stroke my magic puppet," Santa said, "watch what happens."

The little girl did as Santa said.

"It moved!" she squealed with delight.

About five minutes went by. Suddenly, there was a terrible scream from Santa. The store manager rushed in.

"What happened?" he asked.

"Santa's Magic Puppet got real big and red, and then spit in my face," the little girl told him, "so I bit it off!"

***

What does Santa and his reindeer, run over by a train, have in common with a heroin addict?
Track marks.

***

Santa Claus got on a scale. He put in a nickel and out came a card saying, "Come back when you're alone."

***

What's the difference between Santa's sleigh and a UFO?
A UFO doesn't leave a trail of reindeer shit behind

Why is Santa in debt?
He's always in the red.

***

What do you call Santa's sleigh after it was hit by an incendiary device?
An Unidentified Frying Object.

***

A woman came into a police station on Christmas Eve. Her clothes were torn, her face bruised.

"Police, police!" she cried. "I've just been raped by a man dressed as Santa Claus!"

Immediately a detective from the Sex Crimes Squad went up to her, put his arm around her, and said, "There, there. Not to worry. There's no such thing as Santa Claus."

***

How was the airline pilot able to prove he saw Santa flying by?
He found reindeer dung on the wings of his plane.

***

What's red, white, stiff and stuck?
Santa with a hard-on.

***

Why is the fireplace so sticky on Christmas morning?
Because Santa came down the chimney.

Why doesn't Santa go up the chimney anymore?
He doesn't want to get any sexually transmitted diseases.

***

What did the woman moan while having sex with St. Nicholas?
"Santa Claus is coming!"

***

Ever since Santa started messing around with the mothers on his route, Mrs. Claus no longer wears a nightcap to bed — she drinks it.

***

What did Santa say while he was eating out the little girl?
"Yes, Vagina, there is a Santa Claus."

***

How did Santa lose his reindeer and sleigh?
He parked it on a ghetto street.

***

What kind of children go to the express line when they see Santa at a department store?
Kids who want ten toys or less.

***

What did the little girl say when she sat on the department store Santa's lap?
"My, Santa, what a pointy lap you have!"

How do we know that Santa has a foot fetish?
He's into people's stockings.

***

What do you call the flood waters that drowned
Santa and his reindeer?
A yuletide.

***

What's red, white, and blue?
Santa in a porno movie.

***

What do cannibals call Santa Claus?
Christmas Dinner for the whole village.

***

Why did the moron hang a rubber over the fireplace?
He wanted Santa to come.

***

What's red and white and red and white?
Santa wrapped around a barbershop pole.

***

What happened when Santa kissed Mommy?
He got so stiff he couldn't fit back up the chimney.

How does Santa know the rest of us are crazy?
Because there is no Sanity Claus.

***

What's red, white, scorched and travels 400 MPH?
Santa being sucked through the engine of a Boeing 747.

***

What's red and white and flies?
A pizza in Tijuana.

***

How do you know if Santa had an accident on Christmas Eve?
The Yule log in your fireplace smells without burning.

***

What do you call a house where they find the burned and charred body of a fat man in the chimney on Christmas morning?
Santa's last stop.

Christmas Trees, Wreaths, Mistletoe, and Other Sexual Paraphernalia

Chapter Eleven

Why did Pinocchio try to fuck the Christmas tree?
He had an Oedipus complex.

***

What do you call it when the three blind Texas morons tried to cut down a Christmas tree with a power saw?
The Texas Chainsaw Massacre.

***

(Ask a friend): "What's the difference between a Christmas tree and a piece of toilet paper?"
(They answer): "Gee, I don't know."
(You smirk, point your finger, and yell): "So you're the one!"

What does a nerd who jerks off a lot have in common with a decorated Christmas tree?
Shiny balls.

***

What does a newly-cut Christmas tree have in common with a newborn Jewish boy?
They both get trimmed eventually.

***

What did King Kong think the Christmas wreath was?
An organic cock ring.

***

Why do dogs love Christmas?
They can pee on a tree and never leave the house.

***

Why do cats love Christmas?
The whole house smells like pine-scented kitty litter.

***

Why did the nerd hang mistletoe over the kitty litter?
He wanted to kiss some pussy.

***

At an office Christmas party, why did the secretary hang mistletoe under her boss's chair?
She was a little kiss-ass.

What's red and green and pointy?
1. Holly.
2. Poinsettias.
3. Whatever it is, if it's between your legs, you'd better go see a doctor.

Christmas Cards and Seals, or Junk Mail

Chapter Twelve

What's an appropriate Christmas message for one and all?
The middle finger.

***

What's the difference between a NASA seal and a Christmas seal?
Christmas seals usually stick.

***

Christmas Seal: A small furry animal you kill with a Christmas Club.

***

Christmas Card: Someone who writes holiday jokebooks.

Why didn't they put Bo Derek on a Christmas Seal?
They were afraid people would lick the wrong side.

***

How can you tell if a Christmas card comes from an illegal alien?
They never have green ones.

***

What's it called when a yuppie sends a Christmas card?
Networking.

***

What's it called when a nerd sends a Christmas card?
Soliciting.

***

What's it called when a born-again sends a Christmas card?
Proselytizing.

***

What's it called when a nympho sends a Christmas card?
Propositioning.

***

Then there is the Advent calendar for dieters. Every time you open one of the little windows, you see another part of Santa Claus naked. After 25 days of this, you really hate fat bodies.

***

Why are Christmas cards a Catch-22?
If you don't get them, you feel rejected. If you do, you have a mailing list. Bah, humbug!

***

For whom is sending Christmas cards a much more rewarding experience than receiving them.
Hallmark.

Christmas Gifts and Greed

Chapter Thirteen

How can you tell when it's Labor Day?
The first Christmas ad appears on TV.

***

Christmas Gift: Something you have to buy to keep your kids from feeling underprivileged.

***

Christmas: When you buy this year's presents with next year's money.

***

What do parents get at Christmas?
Poorer.

What Christmas gift is far better to receive than to give?
Head.

***

Instead of opening a Christmas Club account, a man decided to save up money by depositing a quarter in a piggy bank every time he fucked his wife. A few weeks before Christmas, when he and his wife were ready to go shopping for gifts, they broke open the piggy bank. To the man's surprise, ten and twenty dollar bills rolled out along with a lot of quarters.

"I don't understand it," the man said, "I put only quarters in there. Where did all the big bills come from?"

"Well," his wife said, "everyone isn't as cheap as you are."

***

What kind of Christmas do you receive when you forget to pay the electric bill?
A cool Yule.

***

A blind man with a seeing-eye dog came into a toy store. He lifted the dog up by its tail and started twirling the animal around his head.

"What are you doing?" asked a horrified salesgirl.

"Don't worry," the blind man reassured her, "I'm just browsing."

What do Irish girls get for Christmas?
Corned beef and Cabbage Patch Dolls.

***

For Christmas, a man sent his mother a parrot that could speak five languages. He called her later to see how she liked the bird.

"It was delicious," his mother told him.

"You mean you ate it!" cried the man. "Didn't you know that that bird spoke five languages?"

"Well," his mother replied, "he didn't say a goddamn word while I was plucking his feathers."

***

Why didn't the nerd join the Christmas Club?"
He didn't think he had time for the meetings.

***

A nympho went into a store to complain about a vibrator she had received as a Christmas gift. The store clerk plugged it in and turned it on.

"It seems to be working fine," he said.

"Oh, it runs okay," the nympho complained, "but every time I use it I chip a tooth."

***

What did the gay say when he got a year's supply of condoms for Christmas?
"Oh boy! Seal-a-Meal!"

What do little Soviet girls get for Christmas?
Red Cabbage Patch Dolls.

***

As a special Christmas present for his elderly wife, an old man arranged for her to be serviced by a handsome, virile young stud. The old woman lay naked on the bed as she watched the hired lover undress. Finally, he was naked except for the condom on his erect penis.

"Oh, how thoughtful," the old woman said. "It's even gift-wrapped!"

***

What Christmas present did the mean old scrooge give the children at the School for the Blind?
Two dozen Rubik's Cubes.

***

What do you call someone who gives Christmas gifts to a mean, flatulent old man?
Generous to a *fart*.

***

What did the gay say when he got an electric blanket for Christmas?
"Oh boy! An electric bun warmer!"

***

Why did the man give his frigid wife six cats for Christmas?

He wanted her to have six appropriate pallbearers for her dead pussy.

***

A man wanted to buy his wife a genuine virgin wool sweater for Christmas.

"How do I know this sweater came from genuine virgin sheep?" he asked the salesclerk.

"I know the Scotsman who raised them," the clerk replied, "and I'm absolutely sure he wasn't into fucking sheep."

***

What did the dissatisfied newlywed bride want to give her husband for Christmas?
About five more inches.

***

What's the difference between a JAP and getting socks for Christmas?
Getting socks for Christmas really sucks.

***

What adult sex toy do rural Greek teenage boys get for Christmas?
Inflatable plastic goats.

***

What did Ronald Reagan give his press secretary for Christmas?
A new manure spreader.

What do greedy kids hang over the fireplace?
Stretch pantyhose.

***

Where did Dracula open his Christmas Club account?
At the blood bank.

***

What do you give an incurable romantic for Christmas?
Penicillin.

***

One Christmas, a man gave his wife a cemetery plot. The next Christmas, he didn't give his wife anything.

"Why didn't you give me a Christmas present this year?" she asked.

"Why should I?" he replied. "You haven't even used what I gave you last year."

***

Christmas is the season when gentlemen befur blondes.

***

What's the difference between Teddy Ruxpin and Ronald Reagan?
Teddy Ruxpin knows more words.

How can you save a small fortune when you go Christmas shopping?
Start out with a large one.

***

What do the CIA and the KGB exchange at Christmas?
Spies.

***

Did you hear about the car the Palestinians gave the Israeli ambassador for Christmas?
It was a real bomb!

***

Why did the cheap man leave the house to call up his wife on Christmas?
She asked for a ring.

***

What Christmas gift for a certain handicapped person is like a North American bird?
A woodpecker.

***

A little boy was obsessed by the idea that he was going to get a pony for Christmas. No matter how hard his parents tried, they couldn't convince him that he wasn't going to get a pony. They lived in an apartment and such a gift would be impractical. But the boy persisted in his delusion, even going so far as to pile up hay in his room and build a little stable in his closet. He told all his friends that he was sure he was going to get a pony and spent a lot of time deciding on a name for the animal. The boy's parents became worried that when Christmas arrived, with no pony, their son would be totally devastated. To avoid any deep mental damage, they decided to take him to a child psychiatrist a few days before Christmas. After examining the boy, the psychiatrist consulted with the parents.

"Your son," he said, "is so fixated by this delusion that only a blatant symbolic gesture on your part will bring him back to his senses. What you should do is leave a large pile of horseshit under the Christmas tree. On Christmas morning he'll realize that you mean business about not getting him a pony."

So, on Christmas Eve, after the boy was asleep, his parents piled a large amount of horseshit under the tree. The next morning, they found their son gleefully digging in the horseshit.

"Oh boy!" he told them ecstatically, "I know there's a pony somewhere under all this shit!"

***

Who got the first Lincoln log for Christmas?
Mrs. Lincoln.

***

A man got an hour with a prostitute as a Christmas present from his boss. She was about to go down on him when the man thought it would be a good idea to check her out for herpes sores.

After a few minutes of this, the prostitute became impatient and said to the man, "Look, mister, don't you know not to look a gift whore in the mouth?"

***

Why is it difficult to pick out a Christmas gift for the Happy Hooker?
What can you get a woman who has had everybody?

***

Why did the moron arrive at the Christmas Eve celebration wearing gloves?
He didn't want to come empty-handed.

***

What's a bargain at Christmas?
A gift that's been marked up only 10%.

***

What did Imelda Marcos get for Christmas?
Three thousand pairs of Odor Eaters.

***

Did you hear about the man who got his wife a mink coat for less than $300?
He bought two steel traps and a rifle.

A boss exchanged his Christmas gift with his secretary. He gave her a mink coat, and she smothered him with beaver.

***

For Christmas, Santa left a lonely drunk an inflated life-size doll of a woman, anatomically correct in every detail. The man stumbled into the room, saw the gift, and started to make passionate love to it. Later a cop found him staggering in the street.

"It wasn't my fault, officer," he cried out. "I fucked her and then I bit her on the thigh. She let out a huge fart, flew around the room, and then dove out the window."

***

What do you call a Cabbage Patch Doll that's been fucked by an elf?
A Stuffed Cabbage Patch Doll.

***

What did the leper find in his stocking on Christmas morning?
His foot.

***

How do you know if a gift was wrapped by a leper?
A tongue is stuck to the Christmas seals.

A man entered the store to buy his friend a Christmas gift. He approached a saleslady behind a counter.

"I'd like to see something nice in silk stockings," he said.

She shook her head. "You know, you fucking men are all alike."

***

While Christmas shopping in a store, a man wasn't sure whether or not to use his credit card.

He went up to a sexy salesgirl and asked, "Do you take anything off for cash?"

"She answered, "For fifty bucks I take off my bra and for another seventy-five I'll throw in a great blow job."

***

A man got his wife an energy-saving washing machine.
A rock.

***

Why did the man give his girlfriend a cake of soap for Christmas?
She told him she wanted something for her neck.

***

What's a good Christmas gift for the man who has everything?
A burglar alarm.

What do you get when you turn Teddy Ruxpin on his stomach?
A bear ass.

***

What do you call it when your girlfriend puts a ribbon around her pussy on Christmas Eve?
A gift box.

Christmas Carols and Georges

Chapter Fourteen

"Twas the night before Christmas,
And all through the house
Not a creature was stirring . . .
Some asshole left the gas on."

***

Why do gays like TV during the Christmas season?
A lot of fairy tales are scheduled.

***

What is the whores' favorite carol?
"Oh *Cum* All Ye Faithful"

***

What did the one-legged ballerina wear when she
danced in the *Nutcracker*?
A one-one.

What do you call the Ku Klux Klan holiday party?
A white Christmas.

***

What do you call a deaf and dumb member of King Arthur's Round Table?
Silent knight.

***

What do you call Sir Lancelot when King Arthur found him screwing Queen Guinivere, then punished him by cutting out his tongue and impaling him on stakes?
Silent knight, holey knight.

***

What do you call it when the chess club caught fire during a Christmas Eve tournament?
Chess nuts roasting on an open fire.

***

What did Scrooge suggest to the Ghost of Christmas Yet To Come?
Extended foreplay.

***

What's the difference between a popular Christmas ballet and a JAP?
One's a "Nutcracker," the other a "ballbuster."

What do you call a gay who works at making Damson Preserves?
A Sugar Plum Fairy.

***

How can you tell it's Christmas in Northern Ireland?
They "Deck the Halls with Bowels of Catholics."

***

What is the official gay Christmas carol?
"Dingle Bells, Dingle Bells!"

***

Why is Ebeneezer Scrooge like a corpse passing gas?
They're both mean old farts.

***

In the Soviet Union, a communist TV weatherman named Rudolf kept predicting rain when it would actually snow. He was so consistently wrong that his wife worried that he would lose his job. She voiced her concern.

"Look," he angrily replied, "Rudolf the Red knows rain, dear!"

***

Which of the Kennedy children is famous for performing Christmas songs?
Carolin' Kennedy.

How come George Washington crossed the Delaware
River on Christmas?
He got a special holiday rate on boat rentals.

***

"Twas the night before Christmas,
and all through the house,
Not a creature was stirring,
. . . they used food processors instead."

The Blasphemous Side of Christmas

Chapter Fifteen

How do we know that the Virgin Mary was Jewish?
She thought her son was God.

***

What's the religious side of Christmas for Americans?
Materialism.

***

Why wasn't Christ born in Southern California?
God couldn't find three wise men or a virgin.

***

What did Joseph first call Mary's story of being made pregnant by God?
"The Immaculate Deception."

How do we know that the fourth Wise Man was Polish?
He didn't make it to the Nativity, did he?

***

How do we know that none of the Three Wise Men were Jewish?
They all bought their gifts retail.

***

What does Gloria Vanderbilt have in common with the Virgin Mary?
They both rode to glory on a little ass.

***

Why did the Virgin Mary stop shaving her underarms after the birth of the Baby Jesus?
She had become a Madonna freak.

***

Why were the "Shepherds in the Fields" the first to spot the Star of Bethlehem?
Shepherds always look up while they're fucking sheep.

***

What controlled substance do you find under the carpet of God's messengers?
Angel dust.

What's black, brown, yellow, or red and kinky and hangs from a Christmas tree?
Angel pubic hair.

***

What were the Baby Jesus' first words?
"This place smells like a barn."

***

What did Mary say to Joseph when she first breast-fed the Baby Jesus?
"God sucks."

***

What did Mary say after she first changed the Baby Jesus' diapers?
"Holy Shit!"

***

What did the Baby Jesus say when he was given myrrh as a gift by one of the Three Wise Men?
"What the fuck is myrrh?"

***

Why did Joseph hang mistletoe all over his donkey?
He wanted someone to kiss his ass.

***

What religious coin is issued at Christmas?
The "J.C. Penny."

Joseph was confused when he learned Mary had become pregnant by immaculate conception. He went to the local rabbi to get a professional opinion.

"Rabbi," Joseph said, "My wife tells me she's pregnant as a result of an act of God. What do you think?"

The rabbi pondered and consulted holy scripture.

"Rain also is an act of God, Joseph," he told the puzzled father-to-be, "but common sense tells us to wear rubbers."

***

While thinking about a name for his newborn boy, Joseph came into the stable to see how his wife and new baby were doing. He stepped on a pile of cowshit, tripped and fell on a rusty nail, got up and then severely banged his head on a low rafter.

"Jesus Fucking Christ!" he exclaimed.

"Good idea, Joseph," Mary told him. "I like everything but the middle name."

X-Rated Xmas

Chapter Sixteen

What's the difference between an office Christmas party and a bank hold-up?
At the hold-up, the women usually are asked to lie face down on the floor.

***

What's oral sex for a scrooge?
Humbug-job.

***

What's anal sex for a scrooge?
Humbuggery.

***

What do you call it when someone pinches your ass at the office Christmas party?
A Christmas goose.

Why did the liberated couple fuck in the Nativity scene on the church lawn?
They wanted to put the "X" back in Xmas.

***

What's the difference between regular Christmas and Greek Orthodox Christmas?
On regular Christmas, you don't fuck goats.

***

What did the nymphomaniac secretary say at the gangbang during the office Christmas party?
"Don't cum yet, ye merry gentlemen!"

***

A woman executive became irate when she learned her male peers were getting higher Christmas bonuses. She stormed into her boss's office and confronted him.

Her boss asked, "Well, will you fuck me for a $25,000 Christmas bonus?"

"I'd have to think about that," the woman replied.

"Will you fuck me for fifty bucks then?" her boss then asked.

The outraged woman screamed, "What do you take me for!"

"We've already established that," the boss replied. "Now we're just haggling over price."

***

Why did Christmas remind the man of his nearly frigid wife?
They both come only once a year.

For years, a secretary had been satisfying the sexual needs of her boss. *Taking Dictation* was their little code word for giving a blow job. At the office Christmas party, the boss introduced his wife to the now tipsy secretary.

"Oh," said the boss's wife, "I've heard my husband say how marvelous you are at taking dictation."

"Yes, I suppose," the secretary replied. "But to tell you the truth, I'd much rather just fuck."

***

What does a man with a 12″ cock have in common with an elaborately decorated fireplace on Christmas Eve?
They're both well-hung.

***

What do department store Santas do during the off-season?
Jerk off while watching *Romper Room*.

***

A man gave his wife $100 to buy Christmas gifts for the gardener, the mailman, and the garbage man.

"But what about the paperboy?" the wife asked.

"Enough is enough," grumped the man.

"Fuck the goddamn paperboy!"

"Okay," his wife said with a smile, "I'll invite him to the party too."

***

Why is Christmas like a night in San Francisco?
A lot of fruitcakes get eaten.

On Christmas Eve, a poor man came into a whorehouse.

"Please, please," he pleaded, "I haven't been fucked in five years, but I only have five dollars. Don't you have a special Christmas rate?"

The Madam took pity on him. "In honor of Christmas," she said, "I'm going to let you take a shot at a very special girl, our very own Virgin Mary."

The man was delighted. He was shown upstairs by the Madam and led into a room. A naked woman was lying on a bed. She had a hairlip and open sores all over her body.

"My God! How do you expect anyone to fuck *her*?" the man cried.

The Madam replied, "Now you know why we call her the Virgin Mary."

***

What do you call a blow job at the computer company's annual Christmas party?
Down time.

***

Yuletide: What you call it when a woman is gagged, bound, and raped on Christmas Eve.

***

A little boy was told to go to bed on Christmas Eve so Santa could visit undisturbed. After he was in bed, the boy's mother invited her boyfriend over for a night of holiday sex. The mad humping awoke the boy.

"Mommy! Mommy!" he cried out from his bedroom, "I hear Santa and his reindeer on the roof!"

Between moans, the mother managed to say, "Go back to sleep or he won't come."

A short while later, the woman let out a terrific yell as she climaxed. Again the little boy was awakened.

"Mommy! Mommy! Was that Santa coming?"

"No," sighed the mother, "Go back to sleep."

But the humping continued.

Once more the little boy called out, "Did Santa come yet?"

Suddenly, the boyfriend bellowed, "No, goddamnit! And if you don't shut the fuck up he may *never* come!"

***

What do candy canes and sore cocks have in common?

The white mixes with the red when they're sucked long enough.

Christmas Pornographies

Chapter Seventeen

FAT NICK'S LAST CHRISTMAS

Twas the night before Christmas
and all through the slums,
Not a creature was stirring,
not even the bums.

***

An O.D.'ed junkie had nodded off a stoop,
but was too gone to notice,
He was lying face down
in dog poop.

***

While uptown in the condos
things were still jumping,
All the hip slick yuppies
still sporting, cavorting, and snorting.

Out on the fire escape
of a luxury flat,
Fat Nick the cat burglar
there calmly sat.

***

When the young couple inside
were stupid and drunk,
Fat Nick came into the condo
with nary a clunk.

***

While Jane the young lawyer
mused on her bonus,
John, the stockbroker
got hard in the penis.

***

Humping and bumping on
that Christmas Eve,
The wildest thing that either
could ever conceive.

***

Was that Fat Nick the cat burglar
had crept into their condo,
And stood over them now,
watching their intercourse mambo.

"Oh my God!" said Jane
with a moan.
"Are you climaxing already?"
asked John with a groan.

***

Jane on her back
could see a fat black,
Smiling down on them both,
with stereo in sack.

***

"Go to it, y'all," said Fat Nick
with a grin,
"Don't mind me none,
I just busted in."

***

"Eke!" yelped Jane with a shriek
When she saw what Fat Nick was doing.
That was enough to interrupt John
and screw up his serious screwing.

***

"What's going on here?" demanded John,
turning around,
His upright pecker now
sagging down to the ground.

"It's okay, man," assured Fat Nick,
his own member now growing.
"Just go back to your fuckin',
I'll soon be goin'."

***

With that Fat Nick grabbed the 21″
deluxe color TV,
Jammed that in his sack and
went for the CD.

***

He went for the wedding silver,
some jewelry, a watch.
Then went up to Jane and
bent down and kissed her sweet swatch.

***

"Now, now," said Fat Nick,
"Don't y'all believe,
'Tis far far better
to give than to receive?"

***

He took some stereo speaker wire
and Yule-tied John,
And then with comely Jane
he really started to get it on.

He fucked her over and over
with his black wand thick.
By the time that Christmas morning was about to
come,
so was the horny cat burglar, Fat Nick.

***

"One more time!" roared Fat Nick,
"before I'm all spent."
He flipped Jane on her belly
and up her chimney he went.

***

Now, by this time broker John
had managed to get free,
And very soon did he flee
from this scene of rape 'n robbery.

***

But John soon returned and with him
brought a cop,
But Fat Nick wouldn't stop,
Since now his mighty pecker
Was taking Jane o'er the top.

***

So the cop took aim and fired,
putting an extra hole in Fat Nick's head.
But Jane kept on with her huffing and bucking,
unaware her Christmas Daddy was dead.

"What a Christmas this has been,"
said John to the still quivering Jane,
"Are you all right, sweet love,
or are you in pain?"

***

"I'm fine," said Jane
with a Presbyterian sigh,
"That sure was a better Christmas gift
than any yuppie money could buy."

***

THE TWELVE DAYS OF CHRISTMAS

On the first day of Christmas,
my true love gave to me . . .
A blow job in the bathroom.

On the second day of Christmas,
my true love gave to me . . .
Two teats to suck,
And a blow job in the bathroom.

On the third day of Christmas,
my true love gave to me . . .
Three French whores,
Two teats to suck,
and a blow job in the bathroom.

On the fourth day of Christmas,
my true love gave to me . . .
Four balling broads,
Three French whores,
Two teats to suck,
And a blow job in the bathroom.

On the fifth day of Christmas,
my true love gave to me . . .
Five cock rings,
Four balling broads,
Three French whores,
Two teats to suck,
And a blow job in the bathroom.

On the sixth day of Christmas,
my true love gave to me . . .
Six sluts a-slumming,
Five cock rings,
Four balling broads,
Three French whores,
Two teats to suck,
And a blow job in the bathroom.

On the seventh day of Christmas,
my true love gave to me . . .
Seven swingers sucking,
Six sluts a-slumming,
Five cock rings,
Four balling broads,
Three French whores,
Two teats to suck,
And a blow job in the bathroom.

On the eighth day of Christmas,
my true love gave to me . . .
Eight twats a-twitching,
Seven swingers sucking,
Six sluts a-slumming,
Five cock rings,
Four balling broads,
Three French whores,
Two teats to suck,
And a blow job in the bathroom.

On the ninth day of Christmas,
my true love gave to me . . .
Nine nymphos screwing,
Eight twats a-twitching,
Seven swingers sucking,
Six sluts a-slumming,
Five cock rings,
Four balling broads,
Three French whores,
Two teats to suck,
And a blow job in the bathroom.

On the tenth day of Christmas,
my true love gave to me . . .
Ten harlots humping,
Nine nymphos screwing,
Eight twats a-twitching,
Seven swingers sucking,
Six sluts a-slumming,
Five cock rings,
Four balling broads,
Three French whores,
Two teats to suck,
And a blow job in the bathroom.

On the eleventh day of Christmas,
my true love gave to me . . .
Eleven lesbians a-licking,
Ten harlots humping,
Nine nymphos screwing,
Eight twats a-twitching,
Seven swingers sucking,
Six sluts a-slumming,
Five cock rings,
Four balling broads,
Three French whores,
Two teats to suck,
And a blow job in the bathroom.

On the twelfth day of Christmas,
my true love gave to me . . .
Twelve strumpets porking,
Eleven lesbians a-licking,
Ten harlots humping,
Nine nymphos screwing,
Eight twats a-twitching,
Seven swingers sucking,
Six sluts a-slumming,
Five cock rings,
Four balling broads,
Three French whores,
Two teats to suck,
And a blow job in the bathroom.

PART IV
NEW YEAR

New Year's Bullshit Resolutions

Chapter Eighteen

New Year's resolution: Something that goes in one year and out the other.

***

A preppie's resolution: Stop having sex once a year.

***

A nerd's resolution: Get the other hand involved in masturbation sessions.

***

A redneck's resolution: Screw fewer pigs and more first cousins.

A survivalist's resolution: Clean gun.

***

A heavy metaler's resolution: Learn the alphabet.

***

A punk rocker's resolution: Say no to everything.

***

A cultist's resolution: Sell more flowers.

***

An evangelist's resolution: Open new Swiss bank account.

***

A Valley Girl's resolution: Shave pubic hair *every* day.

***

A yuppie's resolution: Waste less time on biological functions.

***

A hippie's resolution: Try crack.

Why is a New Year's resolution like a nympho-maniac?
They're both easy to make, but hard to keep.

***

What New Year's resolution did the schizophrenic make?
To pull himself together.

***

As a New Year's resolution, a couple decided to curb their outrageous sexual appetites. Now they only fuck in parked cars.

***

What was the compulsive gambler's New Year's resolution?
He wasn't going to gamble anymore; but he wasn't going to gamble any less, either.

***

What was the busy prostitute's New Year's resolution?
To be more laid back.

***

Sidney Spite's New Year's message to girls who haven't lost their virginity: A girl should use what Mother Nature gave her before Father Time takes it away.

New Year's Eve and Adam

Chapter Nineteen

What's the difference between New Year's Eve and St. Patrick's Day?
On New Year's Eve you can drink until you puke without having to march in a stupid parade.

***

What's the difference between New Year's Eve and Thanksgiving?
On New Year's Eve the turkeys are running around.

***

What's the definition of an alcoholic at a New Year's Eve party?
Someone you can't stand who drinks as much as you do.

How did the preppie woman give her husband an extra erotic time on New Year's Eve?
She held his hand while he jerked off.

***

What three words has everybody heard regarding New Year's Eve and no one knows what the fuck they mean?
Auld Lang Syne.

***

At a New Year's Eve party, a married man had sex with a woman other than his wife. He felt guilty, found his wife, took her to a back room, and admitted that he had been unfaithful.

"Was it Carol?" she asked him.

"I can't tell you," said the man.

"Was it Louise?" asked his wife.

But still the man refused to tell.

"How about Phyllis, was it Phyllis?" tried the wife.

"No, no," replied her husband as he headed out into the party again, "but thanks for the good leads."

***

Where do gay men like to spend New Year's Eve parties?
On their stomachs.

***

What drinks do terrorists favor at New Year's Eve parties?
Molotov Cocktails.

What do lesbian tennis players lap up at New Year's Eve parties?
Martini Navratilovas.

***

After throwing a wild New Year's Eve party, a beautiful rich woman awoke the next morning to find herself naked and tucked in her own bed. Her butler came in the bedroom and said it was he who had put her to bed.

"Thanks," said the woman, "I must have really been on my back last night."

"Actually," the butler replied with a sly grin, "Once on your back, twice on your front, and then you gave me a great blow job in the shower!"

***

How can you tell if someone at a New Year's Eve party is feeling his liquor?
See if his fingers are wet.

***

A guy picked up a girl at a New Year's Eve party and took her home to fuck her. When he took off his pants, the girl saw that his erect cock was nearly four feet long.

"Eke!" she cried on seeing it, "I don't want that huge thing up my cunt. I'll just kiss it, okay?"

"Kiss it?" he queried. "Hell, I can do that myself!"

What's the difference between the Guy Lombardo Orchestra and a moose?
The moose has the *horns* in the front and the *asshole* in the back.

***

A man was driving home drunk from a New Year's Eve party. He lost control of his car and hit a tree. A policeman arrived on the scene and saw right away that the man was drunk.

The cop said, "Hey, buddy, don't you know you can't mix alcohol and gasoline?"

"Sure you can," the drunk replied, "but it tastes like shit."

***

How is an orgasmic woman like a New Year's Eve party?
They both come with noise.

***

At a New Year's Eve party, a wife was concerned that her husband was getting too drunk.

She went up to him and said, "Will you at least stop drinking for me?"

He replied, "Hell, what makes you think I'm drinking for *you*?"

***

Why is the first time Adam screwed Eve like a New Year's Eve?
They both involve turning over a new leaf.

In an apartment building, a man's upstairs neighbors, who were punk rockers, were having a very noisy New Year's Eve party. He called them on the phone to ask them to quiet down, but it was so noisy at the party that no one heard the phone ringing. He took a broom handle and started banging on the ceiling.

The next morning, the man saw one of the punks and angrily asked, "Say, didn't you hear me pounding on the ceiling last night?"

The punk replied, "Oh, that's all right, pal. We were making so much fucking noise you didn't bother us at all."

***

What's the difference between an Irish wake and an Irish New Year's Eve party?
One less drunk.

***

A woman was driving home from a New Year's Eve party. She was obviously drunk, and soon a motorcycle cop pulled her over. Because it was New Year's Eve, he decided to give her a break. Instead of arresting her for drunk driving, he'd ask her for a blow job. He tried to explain this to her, but she didn't understand him. She just kept nodding her head. Then the cop unzipped his fly and pulled out his cock.

"Here we go," she moaned, "Another breathalyzer test!"

How can you tell if a man at a New Year's Eve party is a steady drinker?
See if his hands shake.

***

For a special New Year's treat, a yuppie woman demanded that her husband provide her with a champagne bath. The champagne, of course, was a fine Dom Perignon. So after the woman had enjoyed herself by bathing in it, the cost-conscious husband started to carefully spoon the bubbly back into the bottles. When he was nearly done, he discovered he had a cup of liquid left over. Furious, he poured the liquid back on her.

"It's all urine," he told her.

***

If you're out parking after a New Year's Eve party, be careful. Accidents cause people.

***

Why did the drunk preppie stand in front of the mirror all night while getting sloshed at the New Year's Eve party?
His doctor told him to watch his drinking.

***

While his wife was out of town, a man went to a wild New Year's Eve party where he met an attractive woman. He went back to her place later where they had sex for several hours.

Afterward, he confessed, "I feel so ashamed. After all, I'm a married man."

"I know what you mean," the woman agreed, "but people do worse things. Like me, for example. I knew I had herpes but I still took you home and fucked you."

***

How did the cop know the New Year's Eve reveler he stopped was driving under the influence of alcohol?
He kept tripping over the white line in the middle of the road.

***

Why is a drunk at a New Year's Eve party like an egomaniac?
The both see the world revolving around them.

***

It was exactly midnight at a New Year's Eve party. The lights went out. A man took the opportunity to kiss the woman standing next to him. But he kissed her navel instead of her lips.

"Why did you kiss me there?" asked the woman.

"Well," the man told her, "I just wanted to see which you would open first, your eyes or your legs."

***

What happened when the drunk lost his glasses at the New Year's Eve party?
He had to drink straight out of the bottle.

A man encountered his friend who was staggering down the street, obviously drunk.

"I'm on my way back from a New Year's Eve party," the drunk friend said.

"But New Year's Eve was three weeks ago," the other said.

"Oh yeah?" said the drunk, "I knew it was time to go."

***

What kind of bubbly drink do nerds swallow on New Year's Eve?
Farts in the bathtub.

***

A man got soused at a New Year's Eve party. While wandering home he got lost in a cemetery. He soon passed out on a grave. He awoke the next morning, not knowing if he was alive or dead.

"If I'm alive," he asked himself, "why am I lying on this grave? And if I'm dead, why do I have to pee?"

***

A man met a beautiful young girl at a New Year's Eve party. He took her home and led her to his bed. She quickly stripped off her clothes to reveal a lithe, nubile body.

He was taking off his pants when he thought to ask, "By the way, how old are you?"

The girl giggled and said, "Thirteen."

"Good Lord!" the man said and started to put his pants back on.

"What's the matter?" the girl asked. "Superstitious?"

***

Did you hear about the preppie woman who was so domineering over her husband that at their New Year's Eve party the champagne bottles went "mom" instead of "pop"?

***

Two little boys wanted to get drunk for New Year's Eve. They went into a liquor store to buy a bottle. The store clerk said he couldn't sell them anything because they were far too young.

"But it's for our father," one boy pleaded. "He uses it as a laxative."

After a short while, the boys finally convinced the clerk to sell them the whiskey.

Later that night, the liquor store clerk saw the two boys reeling on the street corner, obviously drunk.

He went up to them and angrily said, "I thought you said the whiskey was for your father to use as a laxative!"

"It is," one of the boys told him. "He'll sure shit when he sees us!"

***

Why didn't the man married to the JAP need a noisemaker at the New Year's Eve party?
He brought his wife with him.

What's it called when a woman feigns pain on New Year's Eve to arouse her sadistic boyfriend?
Sham-pain.

***

A man met a woman at a New Year's Eve party. He maneuvered her towards a back room.

"How about a Happy New Year fuck?" he slobbered.

"Okay," the woman agreed. "Happy New Year, Fuck!"

***

Why is New Year's Eve a special night for whores?
It's the one night they get to blow something else besides cocks.

***

What's the best way to hold your liquor at a New Year's Eve party?
In a glass.

***

Why did the nerd bring a ladder to the New Year's Eve party?
He heard that the drinks were on the house.

***

What kind of girls should wear slacks to a New Year's Eve party?
Well-reared girls.

What's worse than spending New Year's Eve with a bad girl?
Spending it with a good girl.

***

What's the symbolic meaning of the ball dropping on New Year's Eve?
Too drunk to perform.

***

What happened to the man who went to the gallows at midnight on December 31?
He had the first hangover of the New Year.

***

Why does Ronald Reagan like the holiday season so much?
For him it lasts 365 days.

New Year's Dayafter

Chapter Twenty

What's the only thing worse than waking up with your wife on New Year's Day?
Waking up with your wife and your best friend.

***

What do nerds traditionally wake up with on New Year's Day?
Chafed skin and aching wrists.

***

What do nymphos traditionally wake up with on New Year's Day?
A whetted appetite.

How do you get rid of a hangover on New Year's Day?
Kick him or her out.

***

What bowl game is played by the two worst college football teams in the United States?
The Toilet Bowl.

***

Why do so many drunk gays wind up at the Rose Bowl Game on New Year's Day?
They're all looking for a tight end.

***

At the Rose Bowl Game, how can you distinguish the Goodyear blimp from Ed McMahon?
The Goodyear blimp has big letters on it.

***

Two pigeons were flying over the Rose Bowl Game.
    "Look at all those people down there!" said one pigeon.
    The other pigeon disdainfully replied, "Where's your sense of sportsmanship?"

***

What bowl game is played on New Year's Day in San Francisco?
The Fruit Bowl.

Why do they call New Year's Day a traveling day?
Because your head is spinning.

***

What food is traditionally eaten on New Year's Day?
Aspirin.

***

How do you define New Year's Day?
The first hangover of the rest of your life.

***

What's the worst thing about New Year's Day?
Only eleven months till the next holiday season.